CORONA

The War on Global Civil Liberties and the Antichrist Agenda

Bridget S. Howe

9781716731037

Contents

Introduction

I had ordered a cloak for my mother for her birthday in February of 2020, and it was coming from China so she wasn't going to get it on time. I was talking to my coworkers about the cloak when my supervisor looked at me and said, "Do you *really* want it?" It was January. I immediately understood her meaning. *Corona.* "Oh. I didn't think about that. Maybe I don't." My mother was turning 86, and the thought of something like Corona infecting my mother sent chills down my spine. I canceled the order and got her a cloak from someone stateside.

In the weeks to follow reports of the spread of Corona revealed that Corona was no small threat. On March 23rd, I was laid off from work along with multiple other of my coworkers because of the *shelter in place* order given by the Governor of the State of Ohio. On top of that, the Department of Education had suspended our contract at least for the next two months. Our CEO was devastated. My supervisor was in tears, and one of my coworkers was really struggling with it. Ignoring the *social distancing* requirement, I wrapped my arms around my coworker as she burst into tears.

I turned in my badge that day, hoping this wasn't what I thought it was. Unfortunately, as I turned my mind to picking apart Corona, I found exactly what I thought I was going to find. The entire planet was being pulled into the intricate web of the very destructive New World Order. The prognosis of Corona did not look hopeful.

1 History of the Roman Catholic Church

You might be asking yourself what the History of the Roman Catholic Church has to do with the Coronavirus pandemic. My mind works in mysterious ways, but I intend to demonstrate that tactics like deception and fear were used to manipulate and control people in Rome in the same way that deception associated with the Coronavirus pandemic is also being used to induce fear to persuade people to cooperate with a private agenda of an elite few who have power and wealth. These figures are familiar with Roman tactics, believe in the glory of Rome, and are using the same tactics deliberately. My attempt in this book is to alert Americans and the body of believers especially to these tactics so they can recognize them and not be deceived by them.

In 324 AD Christian Constantine became the absolute Emperor of Rome. He allegedly and historically was converted to Christianity and made Christianity the state religion. This is how the Roman Catholic Church was born. How exactly did this come about?

Constantine's *conversion* was in 312 BC. He became Emperor after his father's death. For this, he had to win a war with General Maxentius. Before Constantine became Emperor, the church was hotly persecuted, and Christians were being slaughtered. However, when Constantine made Christianity the state religion, the war against Christianity ceased. But did it? Constantine made a profession of faith. The church fathers believed in his profession of faith. He was thus able to persuade the church fathers to adopt pagan customs and incorporate them into the worship of Yahweh to persuade the pagans to come to church. How clever. However, this would be strictly forbidden in scripture. Nevertheless, the church fathers complied. The day of worship changed from Saturday to Sunday. Sunday was the day the pagan god Rah or Ray the Egyptian Sun god was worshipped. This is the Roman name for the ancient rebel, Nimrod, who implemented fire worship in Babylon. The church ceased celebrating the holidays that Yahweh commanded in the Old Testament such as the Passover etc. and began celebrating Christ's birth on Christmas and on Easter his resurrection. Keep in mind, before this the early church was faithful to Sabbath worship on Saturday and the 7 feast days established by Yahweh with the exodus of the Hebrews from Egypt. The early church did not celebrate a Christmas or Easter Holliday.

Modern Christians believe that we worship God on Sunday because Jesus was raised on Sunday. However, the notion that Jesus was raised on Sunday is disputed by those who understand Jewish holidays and Sabbath celebrations. Also, the Hebrew calendar was lunar and the new day started at sunset and not sunrise. This is the way Yahweh established it. The word Sabbath refers not only to the weekly day of worship but also the seven holidays that Yahweh commanded the Hebrews to celebrate. A good book to review for an alternate view of the Sabbath worship is *Holidays or Holy Days* put out by the United Church of God. Also, a book by Don Esposito called *The Great Falling Away,* and the book by the late pastor Alexander Hislop, *The Two Babylons* are informative and eye-opening. Those who dispute the Sunday worship day believe that Jesus was raised just before sunset on Saturday. Early on the first day of the week, Sunday, Jesus was already raised from the dead. Mary did not see him rising from the dead, she found an empty tomb. Sunset on Saturday in the Hebrew day is the beginning of Sunday. The prophecy that Jesus gave his disciples in Matthew 12:40 indicates exactly how long Jesus would be in the tomb. "And even as 'Jonah was in the belly of the huge fish three days and three nights,' so shall the Son of Man be in the heart of the earth three days and three nights," (Hebrew Roots Bible (HRB)). If he was crucified on Friday and raised on Sunday this prophecy failed. Friday night, Saturday and Saturday night and Sunday Morning don't add up to three days and three nights. If he was crucified on Wednesday and entombed Wednesday evening before sunset, Thursday and Thursday night, Friday and Friday night, and Saturday being raised just before sunset on Saturday would be three days and three nights. Why Wednesday? Because the Passover was being celebrated on Thursday that year. The bodies had to be pulled from the crosses before the Passover celebration began. The Passover is one of Yahweh's Sabbaths. Ergo, there is much support for the conclusion that we worship on Sunday because Constantine was still a pagan sun god worshipper and not a true believer in Jesus Christ.

December 25th is the day Rah, the Sun god, was born and Easter is the day when the ancient Queen Semiramis, the wife of the pagan King Nimrod, *raised* her murdered husband from the dead. Easter is the English version of the name of the pagan god *Ishtar or Istar* which is another name for Semiramis.

That the Roman Catholic church was corrupted is beyond dispute with a long and documented history of treachery murder and mayhem, apart from just persecuting true believers in Jesus Christ. Notwithstanding, during WWII devout Catholics worked at hiding and saving the Jews and their children. We cannot deny that there are devout Catholics who sincerely live out their faith in Jesus Christ and have contributed much to humanitarian causes throughout the world. On the flip side, in the 1400's Catholics also threatened the Jews if they did not raise their children as good Catholics they would take their children away from them. Ergo, there are Jews today who do not know they are Jewish because they were raised Catholic.

Today there are surfacing multiple testimonies from children who were taken to the basement of the Vatican to witness ritual sacrifices on a black stone altar. Thousands of children have been molested by Catholic priests, and the statute of limitations on filing charges for child molestation as been extended for victims of sexual abuse by Catholic priests. There are multiple points in the Catholic faith that points to its pagan origins;

- The Catholic Pope is called the *Vicar of Christ* which means *instead of Christ*.
- The word of the Pope has been asserted to be superior to the word of God.
- An ancient pagan idol, identified as Molech, has been erected now in the courtyard of the Vatican.
- The Exsultet Prayer sung at Catholic masses in English refers to "Christ your son" while in Latin it refers to Lucifer. So in August of 2015, it caused quite a stir

when, in a public ceremony, Pope Francis referred to Lucifer as the Morning Star, a title given to Christ in the scripture.

The acorn does not fall far from the tree. This is what happens when the worship of Yahweh is mixed with pagan idolatry which Yahweh commanded the Jews to never do. In Ezekiel chapter 8, Ezekiel is commanded by Yahweh to dig a hole in the wall of the Temple. Upon digging the hole in the wall he found an opening, and Ezekiel witnessed the priests worshiping idols in the house of Yahweh. In another place, he witnessed women weeping for Tammuz. Tammuz is another name for Nimrod, the ancient hero/rebel who led the people of Babylon into apostasy. Today the Roman Catholic Church is still plagued with idolatry and secret satanic rituals.

The protestant revolution occurred because the Scripture was finally translated into the common tongue of the people. Scholars like William Tyndale and John Wycliff in the 1400's began translating the Bible so the common man could read it. The Catholic priesthood had been lying to the people about what the scripture said, and *they used these lies to manipulate and control the population.* The Catholic Priests objected to the scripture being translated because they said the scripture was too sacred to be read by the common man. With the translation of the scripture into the common tongue of the people, the people could read the scripture for themselves, and the lies were exposed. Roman Catholicism was a works-based faith. If you wanted to go to Heaven, you had to please the Pope. The people were duly informed by their priest that they could not approach God themselves, but they had to go through the priest. They could not be forgiven for their sins unless they did penance. Imagine how the common folk must have felt when they read the scripture for the first time and learned their sins were paid for by the blood of the Lamb, and they were saved by faith in Jesus Christ alone. Imagine the man who never thought God would listen to him, for the first time getting down on his knees and calling on Yahweh in Jesus' name because the scripture said he could. Imagine a people so oppressed by civil and religious authorities living in fear of their lives suddenly understanding that God was on *their* side. Imagine people who found faith in God that motivated them to put their lives on the line for what they believed so that they did not fear being burned at the stake, beheaded, or buried alive. And just imagine the judgment God brought down on the Holy Roman Empire for their hideous oppression of his sheep. The Holy Roman Empire fell because the people put their faith in God instead of the Church.   The corrupted Holy Roman Empire had used the Church to manipulate and control the people with lies and fear until they discovered the truth and were set free. Imagine.

2 The Roman Empire Returns

Some years ago I had a dream which I did not understand at the time. As years passed and I began researching, the meaning of that dream became clear to me. In my dream, there was a war going on. I was dragging people into the church because I thought we would be safe there. I had people down on the floor between the pews in a defensive posture with their hands covering their heads. Suddenly the entire sidewall of the church was blown out, and on the other side of the wall were a bunch of Roman soldiers on horseback. They began dragging people out of the church and conscripting them into labor. I didn't understand. Was Yahweh telling me that there was something wrong with the church or that the church was not a safe place?

When I was a youth, I belonged to a very active youth group in the Nazarene Church. In that group, we were always being taught that Jesus could come back any minute, and we should be watchful for his second coming. In those days we would be looking at the clouds and see something that looked like an angel or even Jesus, and we would get excited. In those days, it was thought that Sun Myung Moon could be the antichrist, and Russia was the terrible big bad enemy of Yahweh.

The years went by. I went to college and graduated. I joined the Army, was discharged, and became a Case Manager for 18 long years. Life went on, the clouds in the sky came and went, and the Lord Jesus had not yet returned. Yet, in my spirit, I knew his coming was at hand. It did not appear to be at the forefront of everyone's mind, however. People weren't watching the sky anymore. One day on exiting my house in Apple Valley, I had a strange feeling as I looked at my surroundings. I had two lots in Apple Valley. I had a woods and several perennial flower gardens planted around my property. I could stand in my driveway and look down a the sparkling lake. It was beautiful, but something inside of me sensed that it was all fake - a deception. It was as if Yahweh was trying to pull back the curtain and show me what was behind. I said, "Show me. Let me see what we are not seeing. I know it's here somewhere. I know the end is near, but show me." Shortly thereafter I realized that I was being targeted by gang-stalkers and that my employer, the local sheriff's department, and probably my church was also involved. My life was under heavy attack, and no one would listen to me. That was when the Holy Spirit sent me to the library to do some research. What I found was shocking as I spent the next four years researching *If the West Falls* . . . which I published in 2011. I had a fierce struggle with covert operators who were trying to keep me from publishing that book.   I went through four laptops and several printers trying to get that book researched and published. They would lockdown my keyboard so I couldn't type. They changed the password on one laptop and reprogrammed the macros so I couldn't access it anymore. One laptop crashed after 6 months. I never went on the web with any laptop, and they still hacked through. They stole ink from my printer and spilled in on my carpet. They erased the printer drivers from my laptop. They sabotaged the manuscript and my footnotes over and over again. Imagine having to reset 900 plus footnotes in a 400-page manuscript.   All told I spent $5000 on the publication of the book, half of which was for trying to get out the errors they put in the manuscript.

There is something very important that I discussed in that book. It is the key to understanding the political climate of the entire world. George Wilhelm Frederick Hegel who died in 1831, was a professor of philosophy at the University of Berlin. He did not believe in any notion of right or wrong nor any religion or morality. He believed that man is subordinate to the state and finds fulfillment in obedience to the state. He was a Freemason and espoused the Freemason rationalist theology that "reason is the candle of the Lord."[1]   He believed that change is brought about by the resolution of crises. Significant historical figures such as Karl Marx, Adolf Hitler, Meyer Rothschild, Wilhelm Wundt, and Adam Weishaupt applied what became known as the *Hegelian Dialectic* in bringing about about political changes that furthered their agenda which was the establishment of a one-world government. The Hegelian Dialectic states that a force (thesis) dictates its own opposing force (antithesis). These forces in conflict result in the creation of a third force: a synthesis.

They didn't have to wait for a crisis to present itself,

---

1   The obelisk is a Freemason symbol. It is this Freemason symbol that is standing in Washington called the Washington Monument. The obelisk is a symbol of the Sun God Rah (Ray). It is also a symbol of the phallus or male sexual energy.

they would secretly create a crisis and then offer a solution which of course involved changes they wanted to make in the first place. The crisis was designed to persuade the general population that the changes were necessary *for their safety.* Those changes benefitted the wealthy and powerful always strengthening their position. So when the European bankers wanted to put Hitler in power and depose the current chancellor of Germany, ***Kurt von Schleicher,*** they created a crisis. One of their agents set fire to the Reichstag and blamed the fire on a mentally retarded youth. Suddenly the safety and security of the entire State were at risk and w-la, Hitler suddenly becomes the chancellor of Germany deposing the former chancellor.

This same kind of thing happened in Russia when Boris Yeltsin wanted a particular former KGB agent to become the President of Russia. Yeltsin, in an attempt to promote Democracy in Russia, had illegally given away state assets to friends. These friends became oligarchs who further impoverished the people of Russia. When the new President of Russia was elected and took office, the crime would be discovered. However, Yeltsin had a healthy relationship with Vladimir Putin who he knew would not send him to prison if he was elected to the office of President. But Vladimir Putin was not well known to the population of Russia. However, amazingly and quite conveniently, in September of 1999, several apartment house bombings created a significant crisis. Three hundred died and 1000 were injured and fear and panic spread. Vladimir Putin was put in charge of the investigation. His handling of the crisis made him a hero in the eyes of the voters. Several months later he is elected President of Russia.

We see this same, "order out of chaos" theme in the politics of the US over and over again. What occurred on September 11th in 2001 is certainly another crisis created so that those in power could make major policy changes without the citizens of the US objecting too much. Interestingly, George W. Bush also made a profession of faith in Christ (as did Yeltsin). That effectively gave him the evangelical community on a platter. So, did the evangelical community ever question the official story of what happened on September 11th, 2001? Sadly, I am still hearing pastors standing behind the pulpit talking to their congregations about those Muslim terrorists who attacked America on September 11th. This even though multiple very intelligent and highly qualified professionals in their fields have effectively debunked the 9/11 lie several times over. 9/11 was an inside job, and the evidence reveals that the Bush administration was behind the 9/11 attacks. The evidence was so compelling that several lawsuits were levied against the Bush administration by eyewitnesses present on-site during the 9/11 attacks who knew that the official story was a lie. Apparently, the legal system was on Bush's side because, despite overwhelming evidence, the lawsuits failed. But here is our Hegelian Dialectic at work again. In October of 2001, the 400 page Patriot Act document was handed to congress and they were asked to vote on it. No one was allowed to review the document before the vote. The Patriot Act had a devastating impact on our Constitution and our Bill of Rights. The Military Commissions act came in on the heels of the Patriot Act which annihilated the rights of POWS and gave sweeping powers to interrogators whose subsequent abuse of those who were detained because of 9/11 became a scandal. Never has any US military personnel been excused for nor permitted to sexually assault or otherwise torture a POW to get information. This was an absolute disgrace and reflected very poorly on the US Military around the world. The abuses heaped upon innocent civilians at both Abu Ghraib and Guantanamo were an absolute violation of our constitution, our military training, and international law. We were in gross violation of the Geneva Convention. The 9/11 event was the crisis that was designed to upend our Constitution, our Bill of Rights, and our common sense with it.

After the 9/11 crisis, multiple arrests of Muslim peoples who had done nothing wrong resulted in violations of the US Law, the Geneva Conventions, and long-held traditions regarding the treatment of prisoners of war. What it boiled down to is the fact that 9/11 was an inside job. The official story of what happened on 9/11 was an absolute fabrication, and there were multiple witnesses to that fact. However, since the official story was that we were attacked on 9/11 by Muslim terrorists, they had to make a good show of it. Ergo, they arrested innocent civilians who had done nothing wrong, tortured them to get false confessions, denied them their legal rights, etc. The situation was so disparaging that several prosecutors involved in the situation resigned. Contrary to long-standing due process laws, no evidence was needed to get a conviction and hearsay evidence was allowable. The Chief Prosecutor, Colonel Morris Davis, resigned when the Department of Defense General Counsel William Haynes was placed over him in the chain of command. Haynes had insisted that they could not acquit anyone.[2]

In sum, the Bush Administration perpetrated a crime against the American people resulting in the deaths of 3000 Americans. They blamed it on Muslim terrorists. To validate the lie they arrested multiple Muslims who had done nothing wrong, denied them proper due process, and tortured them to get false confessions.

---

2   David Ray Griffin, The New Pearl Harbor Revisited: 9/11, The Cover-up and the Expose (Northampton: Olive Branch Press, 2008) 215 -218.

Evangelicals need to be very concerned about the deception involved in 9/11 perpetrated by an administration whose Executive made a profession of faith in Jesus Christ. This is exactly what Constantine did. It was a lie designed to soften Christians and gain their cooperation. The church was prepared to cooperate because it was for our *safety*. What does the scripture say?

> 1 Thessalonians 5:3-4 (HRB) For when they say, Peace and safety! Then suddenly destruction comes upon them, like the travail to the woman with child, and not at all shall they escape. But you, brethren, are not in darkness, that the Day should overtake you as a thief.

Do we need to be reminded that it was the prophets' job to hold the king accountable? It was Nathan the prophet's job to confront King David with his sin. Jeremiah likewise faced the same challenge. Jeremiah spoke the words that neither the King nor the people nor the *priesthood* wanted to hear. He suffered for it, but he did his job.

This year, in March the country went into lockdown status in response to the Coronavirus crisis. Is this another manmade crisis to enact another part of the plan to implement the New World Order? Does it follow a pattern? Let's take a look at this "crisis."

The word *on the street* is that Corona is a fake crisis. The number of deaths resulting from Corona is substantially minimal compared to other flu crises we have experienced such as the bird flu, the swine flu, SARS and N1H1, etc. However, honest medical professionals have reported that anything and everything is being called as a Corona casualty. So if you died of a heart attack, it is reported as complications from Corona.

Minnesota Senator Scott Jensen, who is also a physician, reveals that the American Medical Association is encouraging doctors to classify something as COVID-19 even if there is no test showing any diagnosis of COVID-19. Jensen received a 7-page document that showed him how to fill out a death certificate as a "COVID-19 diagnosis" even when there isn't a lab test confirming the diagnosis. He states in an interview with Fox News,

> Right now Medicare is determining that if you have a COVID-19 admission to the hospital you get $13,000. If that COVID-19 patient goes on a ventilator you get $39,000, three times as much."[3]

Dr. Ngozi Ezike, Director of the Illinois Department of Public Health, has reported the same thing also saying that 90% of patients who died reportedly of COVID-19 were patients who had some other underlying medical condition. She reported that a death is listed as caused by COVID-19 even if there are clear indications of an alternative cause. In the UK the same problem exists.   Medical professionals indicate that when a death is listed as COVID-19, there is nothing to say they would not have died anyway of alternative causes.[4]

What has happened since the shut-down and what will the shut down accomplish?   This is a dangerous economic maneuver for both families and businesses. It could result in many being drained of their financial resources especially since

---

3   Wayne Dupree, US Hospitals Getting Paid More to Label Cause of Death as 'Coronavirus' (Subterranean Homesick News, globalresearch.ca, April 15, 2020)

4   Arjun Walls, "If you die of a clear alternative cause, it's still listed as a COVID death." - Dr. Ngozi Ezike (collective-evolution.com, April 25, 2020).

many have been laid off from their jobs. Businesses are not able to function as usual which is going to impact their ability to remain viable. So if people are running out of resources, that limits their ability to respond appropriately to this crisis and being drained of resources they are also drained of power. That will make them more dependent on the government to survive. That is a danger signal. To accommodate the financial burden, the government is handing out stimulus checks and offering small business loans to support businesses in the crisis, which is surely appreciated by the American public. However, where is this money coming from? It this ultimately going to result in financial hardship for those on Social Security? If not then where is it coming from? Did the Federal Reserve just print more money? Our concern should be how this is going to affect the economy and financial well being of all Americans in the long run.

3 Corona and Bill Gates

Consider that Bill Gates has been in the middle of this Coronavirus pushing the vaccine along with a microchip which will be implanted with the vaccine. Who is Bill Gates? He's the world's number 1 computer geek. He's not a medical doctor. So why would someone who is involved in the development of computers, software, and internet systems be so heavily invested in creating a vaccine for a virus? Not to mention the fact that he is not an elected official? What is his interest in this? Have you asked yourself?

The answer to that begins with an idea that surfaced in 1883 when Sir Francis Galton published *Inquiries Into Human Faculties and its Development* in which he first mentioned the topic *eugenics*. The term comes from the word eugenes which means *well-born*. The idea of creating a master race of royal blood caught fire, and institutions such as the Kaiser Wilhelm Institute and the Cold Spring Harbor Institute were created and funded to encourage people to accept the idea. It became an academic discipline by the 20th century. Margaret Sanger founded Planned Parenthood to promote the eugenics agenda. Thomas J Watson, head of IBM, established Watson Business Machines in Poland to aid the Nazi invasion of Poland. Watson continued to aid Hitler in the war, and the entire operation was managed from IBM Headquarters in New York. Thomas Watson passed the business on to his son, Thomas Watson jr., who's daughter married Margaret Sanger's grandson, Alexander Sanger. The entire impetus behind the Holocaust was the idea of creating a master race and purifying the gene pool by destroying the lives of inferior peoples.

Bill Gates' father worked on the board of Planned Parenthood, and his mother worked on the corporate board for IBM. Bill Gates partnered with IBM to create Microsoft. He has no medical background, but he went on to become the world's number one promoter of vaccines and population control. Bill Gates funds the World Health Organization (WHO) and the Center for Disease Control (CDC) among other NWO organizations.

Dr. Anthony Fauci is on the president's Coronavirus response team and also on the leadership council of the Bill and Melinda Gates Foundation. In January 2017 Dr. Fauci told an audience at Georgetown University that there would be a surprise outbreak during the Trump presidency. Georgetown U is a very expensive private school where the wealthy and powerful send their children to be educated. Then in October of 2019 Bill Gates sponsored event 201, a simulation that estimated 65 million people killed by the Coronavirus. In November of 2019, the Bill Gates-funded Pirbright Institute was granted a patent for the Coronavirus vaccine that could be used on humans.[5] This is very interesting since the first indication of

---

5   Greg Reece, SHOCKING! HISTORIAN EXPOSES BILL GATES' TIES TO NAZIS AND MORE: YouTube, Infowars, bitchute.com, April 8th, 2020).

the Coronavirus threat was discovered in *December 2019*.[6]

Gates is a billionaire, and his philanthropy is a means to exert influence over the organizations he contributes to, especially if their budget becomes dependent on those funds. Gates had donated huge sums of money to the WHO, and what is the WHO notorious for?

> *... since 1973 the World Health Organization has been looking for ways to use vaccines and injections to control the world's fertility. If those methods are offered to men and women so that they can make a choice about their reproductive lives, well and good. If, however, they are hidden in smallpox vaccines (Africa) with the avowed purpose of "eliminating 150 million excess Sub Saharan Africans" as they were in vaccines distributed by the WHO starting in 1985, or in tetanus vaccines which would cause abortions in South and Central America women starting in the 1990s, we are not dealing with reproductive options, but reproductive genocide.[7]*

In addition to the WHO, in 2010 the Bill and Melinda Gates Foundation purchased shares in the Monsanto corporation to the tune of 500,000 with a value upwards of $23 million.[8] What is Monsanto known for? Besides making genetically modified vegetables, herbicides that reduce production and cost farmers more money not to mention putting farmers at risk for developing cancer, Monsanto was behind the production of spermicidal corn seed sold to Mexican farmers. They sold corn seed to Mexican farmers that contained a spermicidal agent that killed sperm in Mexican males who ate the corn. Corn is a

---

6   Staff Writers and wires News.com AU, China Knew about Coronavirus weeks before outbreak, (news.com.au, March 3, 2020, 08:56 am).

7   Joseph Plummer, Sterility and Spermicidal Corn, (josephplummer.com).

8   ibid

staple in Mexico. The entire future of Mexico could have been completely decimated!

Clearly, all reports indicate that the Bill and Melinda Gates Foundation is pushing population control including supporting the NWO agenda to reduce the world population. Their foundation has funded the WHO which pushed vaccinations on third world nations who were not asking for them. Many nations have accused the WHO of poisoning their population with vaccines causing death, disease, and sterilization.   Most recently the WHO and Bill Gates were kicked out of India because 490,000 children suffered from a non-polio acute flaccid paralysis (NPAFP) after receiving a Gates sponsored vaccine regime between 2000 and 2017. After their being pushed out of the country the number of NPAFP cases dropped.[9] An article published by the research team in India by Dhiman, Prakash, and Puliyel did show a significant causative relationship between the increase in the number of NPAFP cases and the rounds of the vaccine distributed by WHO.[10] You decide.

---

9   Mark Zorn, Robert Kennedy Jr. Exposes Bill Gates and His Globalist Vaccine
    Agenda (Visionlaunch Media, visionlaunch.com; April 16, 2020.
10 Rachana Dhiman, Sandeep C. Prakash, [...], Sandeep C. Prakash, Correlation
    between Non-Polio Acute Flaccid Paralysis Rates with Pulse Polio Frequency in
    India (ncbi.nlm.nih.gov, August 15, 2018.

4 Using Fear as a Weapon

I have discussed already that our government is using the "Order out of Chaos" model, a crisis used to induce fear to persuade people to cooperate with changes that are *not* in their best interests. If the Corona pandemic is another lie, then the face mask, social distancing, and shelter in place orders have another agenda. We have already discussed how the figures related to deaths from COVID-19 are grossly inflated. A deceptive tactic is being used to induce fear.

In addition to this, the CDC and Surgeon General Dr. Jerome Adams have indicated that wearing a mask is not necessarily going to have any impact on the spreading of the virus. An article published on the Business Insider web page states,

> There isn't much good evidence that masks help prevent infection from spreading in a population, except when you put them on the people who are

already sick. There are also risks associated with wearing a homemade mask: You might just be turning your scarf into a virus-catcher.[11]

An article from Live Science indicates wearing a mask *may* help prevent the spreading of the virus. The N95 mask is the most effective against spreading disease, however, these are used by medical professionals and are in short supply even for them. The mask only prevents about 10% of the air around you from penetrating. The rest moves through or around the mask. There is little to no effect against spreading disease, so it is not wise to rely on a mask.[12] Even the WHO does not recommend wearing a mask.

- There is currently no evidence that wearing a mask (whether medical or other types) by healthy persons in the wider community setting, including universal community masking, can prevent them from infection with respiratory viruses, including COVID-19.

- WHO does recommend special masks (N95 masks or equivalent) plus other protection for health-care workers working with people who have, or are suspected to have, COVID-19.[13]

---

11 Hilary Brueck, The CDC is recommending that people wear face coverings or cloth masks if they go out in public (Business Insider, businessinsider.com, April 3rd, 2020 5:44 pm.)

12 Stephanie Pappas, Live Science Contributor, Do face masks really reduce coronavirus spread? Experts have mixed answers. (Live Science, livescience.com, April 12, 2020)

13 PAUL GLASZIOU & CHRIS DEL MAR, THE CONVERSATION, Should We All Be Wearing Face Masks? Here's Why Experts Are So Conflicted, (Science Alert, sciencealert.com, April 9, 2020).

If the WHO and the CDC are under Gates' influence, I wouldn't be interested in listening to them anyway. If medical professionals are conflicted about wearing masks, but no real data showing that wearing a mask is effective in preventing the spread of disease, why are we wearing them.? Is it not another method of spreading fear or another method for exerting control over our behavior?

Dr. Judy Mikovits, an accomplished microbiologist and medical researcher who in 1991 published her doctoral thesis that revolutionized the treatment of aids patients. As a former employee of Dr. Anthony Fauci, she later published an article in the Journal of Science that shocked the medical community. In her article, she reveals how animal and fetal tissues present in vaccines were unleashing devastating plagues and chronic diseases on the population. Big Pharma went after her with a vengeance. She was arrested without a warrant and held five days without being charged with a crime. She was given a 5-year long gag order. In an interview with Mikki Willis of wcntv.net, she explains that Dr. Tony Fauci. who is head of the President's Corona Task Force and also head of the National Institute of Allergy and Infectious Disease, directed the cover-up and paid off those who could have supported Dr. Mikovits to the turn of millions of dollars. Dr. Mikovits was denied her due process rights.[14] She has recently published a book, *Plague of Corruption,* in which she discusses lies perpetrated by those in the medical community regarding contagions.

When I googled Judy Mikovits, I found all kinds of articles accusing her of being a conspiracy theorist. I regularly search the web for information on any given topic. I am very familiar with the term *conspiracy theory*. A theory is something

___

14 Mikki Willis, Dr. Anthony Fauci's ex-employee, was jailed, finally tells all (WCNTV, wcntv.com).

that has not been tested. A theory is a statement of what one believes to be true. This is followed by a hypothesis which is a concrete method of testing the theory to see if it is valid. For example, I can examine the plants in my house all of which appear to be wilting. My theory is that they don't have enough water. I develop my hypothesis which states that if I put more water on my plants they will perk up. If I put more water on my plants, and they do perk up, then I have proven my theory. One of the other aspects of testing a theory is that the experiment has to be able to be replicated. So if someone else has plants in their house that are also wilting, they will take my theory, apply the hypothesis, water the plants, etc to see if they get the same results. Once the theory has been tested several times by multiple people using the same methods as the original and getting the same results, the *theory* is proven to be true. At that point, it is no longer a theory. It is an established fact. One of the most prominent examples of this is the theory that doctors were passing germs from one patient to another resulting in multiple deaths. A Hungarian doctor, Ignaz Semmelweis, first introduced the idea in the mid-1800s and insisted that washing your hands was necessary to prevent this from happening. It made him very unpopular in the medical community because he was implying that doctors were the cause of their own patients' deaths. However, as time passed several doctors made the same observation and hand washing became standard practice.

What happens when those committed to establishing the New World Order don't like someone exposing their lies, they brand them a *conspiracy theorist*. It is very interesting to me that Robert F. Kennedy Jr. wrote the forward to Dr. Mikovits's book in which he discussed the multiple medical professionals, all experts in their field and very credible witnesses, who were also likewise discredited by the *opposing force* in the medical field including Big Pharma. It was President John F. Kennedy who first alerted us to the *Conspiracy* in the first place, and this is likely one of the reasons why he was assassinated. He said in a public address on April 27th, 1961;

> For we are opposed around the world by a monolithic and ruthless conspiracy that relies primarily on covert means for expanding its sphere of influence--on infiltration instead of invasion, on subversion instead of elections, on intimidation instead of free choice, on guerrillas by night instead of armies by day. It is a system which has conscripted vast human and material resources into the building of a tightly knit, highly efficient machine that combines military, diplomatic, intelligence, economic, scientific and political operations.

> Its preparations are concealed, not published. Its mistakes are buried, not headlined. Its dissenters are silenced, not praised. No expenditure is questioned, no rumor is printed, no secret is revealed. It conducts the Cold War, in short, with a war-time discipline no democracy would ever hope or wish to match.

When I review the material on the web of those trying to discredit Dr. Mikovits, she is being called a *conspiracy theorist*. The term implies that the information promoted by the said person is not proven. Yet, Mikovits has several colleagues she has worked with and the attorney and co-author of her book, Kent Heckenlively, JD who would agree with her. The term *conspiracy theorist* also suggests that said person is a *crackpot*. However, Dr. Mikovits could not be considered a *crackpot* by any stretch of the imagination. She was the top scientist in her field. The interview with Mikki Willis reveals just how treacherous the field of medical research can be. It is shocking to think that persons who have sworn to uphold the Hippocratic oath could be so ruthless and devious.

Mikovits is currently speaking out because she knows that millions of lives are at stake because of the propaganda spread by Dr. Anthony Fauci.   She reports that if the Coronavirus vaccine is pushed on the global population those who make the vaccine and who own the patent stand to make millions of dollars, but it will kill millions of people. Coronavirus is not a naturally occurring virus.   It was manipulated in the lab.   She reported that when she was working with Dr. Fauci, they actually trained the Ebola virus to infect humans, otherwise the virus would not have infected humans at all. This is what laboratory manipulation is capable of.[15]

3.7 million dollars was transferred from the National Institute of Health in the US to the Wuhan Laboratory where the outbreak first occurred. Dr. Anthony Fauci had been involved in conducting experiments at that laboratory with the Coronavirus.[16]

When the adherents to the NWO are pushing a hidden agenda, there are always telltale signs that something is wrong. The fact that multiple medical professionals are telling us that they are being told to inflate the figures for deaths from COVID-19 is a telltale sign. The other one is their insistence that everyone has to have this vaccine. Even Anthony Fauci admits that there is no guarantee that the vaccine will work and that it may make things worse.   A drug called

---

15 ibid
16 ibid

Hydroxychloroquine that is regularly used to treat Malaria has been found to be the most effective drug to also treat COVID-19 and has been used around the world successfully. It has been on the list of essential medicines for 70 years. Donald Trump was taking this drug as a preventative measure. However, doctors are being told not to use this drug. A Dr. in Dallas Texas, Yvette Lozano, has been treating patients diagnosed with COVID-19 with Hydroxychloroquine and Azithromycin. It costs $13. It is not a vaccine. The doctor implemented the protocol for treating COVID-19 because that is what Donald Trump said to do. Dr. Lozano's patients improved within 24 hours and were completely recovered within 48 hours.[17] Another COVID-19 patient by the name of Jim Santilli was interviewed by Laura Ingram of Fox News on March 31st, 2020 about his own experience with Hydroxychloroquine and Azithromycin. He had been in the hospital for several days. All sorts of treatments had been tried and he was not getting any better. He was sure he was close to death. Then they brought in a doctor who specialized in infectious diseases who proscribed Hydroxychloroquine and Azithromycin. The treatment had a dramatic effect and within hours he was completely back to normal. On the flip side, A friend of mine had an acquaintance who was diagnosed with COVID-19. who was also treated with the Hydroxychloroquine/Azithromycin combination, and she died. However, they also put her on a ventilator. Dr. Mikovits reported in her interview with Mikki Willis that a ventilator will kill a patient who has COVID-19.

There is one other important fact we all need to know about vaccines. They don't fall under the same laws as malpractice. In other words, if you take their vaccine and it

---

17 Dallas Doctor Yvette Lozano Treating Patients w/ Hydroxychloroquine and Azithromycin. (Big Sky Media, youtube.com, May 15, 2020).

makes you sick or even kills you or a loved one, you have no recourse. You can't sue the doctor who gave it to you nor can you sue the pharmaceutical company. So while drug companies are pushing the vaccine, and those like Bill Gates who invest in their companies stand to make billions of dollars, the vaccine could be making people sick and or killing them, and there is no way to hold them accountable. How convenient.

What is being done is creating an atmosphere of fear which makes thinking for yourself unpopular and risky. They will tell you that if you don't wear a mask you could get infected with the virus. However, you know that qualified professionals have said the opposite. But because everyone else is wearing masks and people are being pressured to wear a mask, you give in a wear a mask. The same goes for social distancing and sheltering in place.

Other measures such as social distancing may harm your immune system. Dr. Dan Erickson, co-owner of Accelerated Health in Bakersfield California, has also indicated that sheltering in place harms on your immune system. The problem is that your immune system is strengthened by exposure to germs and viruses. This is exactly how an infant's immune system is built. He crawls around on the floor, puts his fingers in his mouth, and his immune system is learning to fight disease.[18] This might be disputed by other medical professionals, but research indicates that loneliness can weaken your immune system.[19] Social distancing can harm your emotional well being. It is also harming church congregations. People need affection and touch to be emotionally healthy.

18 Greg Reese, SHELTER IN PLACE' IS WEAKENING THE IMMUNE SYSTEMS OF EVERYONE WHO COMPLIES (Infowars, April 25th, 2020; infowars.com).
19 Axel Schmidt, Reuters Fact Check, Partly false claim: Staying at home and wearing a face mask weakens the immune system (reuters.com).

Touch can also be linked to physical well being. Practicing social distancing has another agenda as well. It may likely have the effect of breaking down relational ties. Bonding and attachment have a lot to do with emotional well being, our ability to function in a healthy way as well as our physical health. Emotional attachments give us strength and energy to fight when our world is turned upside down. The Luciferian elements of our culture are well aware of this. Breaking down social relationships particularly where churches are concerned, actually serves to strengthen their cause. This is the New World Order in action.

5 Corona Agenda

The secret operation, Project Blue Beam, was first made public by a Canadian Investigative Journalist Serge Monast in 1994. This project was designed to bring the world's population into submission to the One World Religion and One World Government headed by the Antichrist. Two years after Monast went public with Project Blue Beam, he died of a heart attack. His associates believed that he was murdered by the CIA.   Project Blue Beam consisted of 4 stages resulting in the population being unable to resist acceptance of the New World Order (NWO). He makes an interesting note that organizations like the World Health Organization, The World Bank, The World Food Program, and the World Trade Center are all organs of the NWO. The FED or Federal Reserve has subjected the world's economics to world control. Big business is all connected to this as well and Big Pharma.   Bill Gates' agenda for population reduction is a part of Project Blue Beam. Bibliophiles states,

The result will be a global empire of the Antichrist, who will rule with the help of his disciples, who would have prepared the grounds to make his reign possible. They will seize all resources and reduce the world population to about one billion by causing natural catastrophes, bloody wars, crushing famines and *devastating epidemics* [emphasis mine].[20]

What is happening since this pandemic was declared is that Bill Gates, *who is not an elected official nor a physician*, seems to be calling the shots. How is it that world leaders are bending to the will of a bully billionaire? Certainly *we the people* did not give him any such authority. Because of the Coronavirus scare, businesses are being forced to close down, people are not permitted to go to work and they are relying on other resources to survive such as savings, retirement funds, and or unemployment. To support Americans during the lockdown, the Cares act was signed into law on March 27 releasing two trillion dollars of funds to those on unemployment and offering small loans to businesses to accommodate for the loss of revenue. Some people were fortunate enough to remain employed if they were considered essential personnel, or were able to work from home. However we don't know how long this will last, and loaning businesses money to keep functioning causes debt which the business will have to repay. The biggest danger is that people will be drained of their financial resources making them dependent on the government. If people have no other resources but the US Government or the Global Government, how are they going to resist when they are being ordered to take a vaccine or microchip? It sounds to me like

20 Aidan Bibliophilius, PROJECT BLUE BEAM - The Quest For A New World Order And The Rule Of The Antichrist. Kindle Edition. (© Copyright 2012 – Aidan Brophilius) Location 101.

Bibliophiles is correct.

In addition to that, the states have been in lockdown status making it impossible for family members to travel to see each other and or provide needed support. Shelter in place orders have locked people at home except for essential trips to the grocery store. Even doctor's offices have been closed down. As we have already discussed people in hospitals are being falsely diagnosed with COVID-19 inflating the figures. More disturbing is that those who are hospitalized and in nursing homes have been isolated from family members and friends.

One of the most telltale signs of a hidden agenda is that church congregations are no longer able to meet due to the *social distancing* policy. A sign posted outside of a church declares that abortion clinics are still open but churches are closed.` Recently the state of California banned singing in church. The American Center for Law and Justice is preparing to fight this violation of our first amendment rights. They are prepared to take this to the supreme court.[21] Not only that, but even as restrictions are lifting we are being told that Corona will always be a threat. So now we have the *war on terror* and *COVID-19 al*ways hanging over our heads.

The worst possible scenario is on the horizon though, with Bill Gates insisting that everyone has to be vaccinated and microchipped. The threat is such that if you are not vaccinated or chipped you will not be able to go to work or buy or sell anything. Evangelicals will recognize this as the mark of the beast and rightfully so. This is clearly what the scripture says will happen toward the end. Already many are insisting that they will not be vaccinated nor chipped.

Revelation 13:16 - 18 (HRB) And the small and the

---

21 Logan Sekulow, Don't Ban Singing in Church (ACLJ.org, July 7, 2020).

great, and the rich and the poor, and the freemen and the slaves, it causes that they give to them all a mark on their right hand, or on their foreheads, even that not any could buy or sell, except the one having the mark, or the name of the beast, or the number of its name. Here is wisdom: Let him who has understanding compute the number of the beast, for it is the number of a man and its number is six hundred and sixty six.

The microchip has been researched and used in experiments for years. During the Viet Nam era, soldiers were injected with the Rambo chip. With this chip, someone sitting behind a computer screen could monitor the soldier's bodily functions, central nervous system, circulatory system, etc. The observer on a computer could also observe everything the soldier was seeing and hearing. His emotional reactions to his environment could also be monitored along with his thoughts. The evil part of this is that what the soldier experienced was recorded and could be played back causing the soldier to re-experience painful traumatic events. It is highly probable that much of what we called PTSD was electronically induced. If this kind of technology existed during the Viet Nam era, think of how much more advanced the technology is now.

The CIA has been experimenting with methods of mind control and behavior control since just after world war II with the help of NZAI scientists. Keep in mind that the scientists were brought to the US after the war after expunging their criminal records where the Jews were concerned. The CIA was interested in their scientific expertise.   This was known as Project Paperclip.

The first problem with microchip technology is that it

takes all your privacy away. You can't have a private thought ever. It is all being recorded. With Directed Energy Weapons (DEW) this is also possible.   Your thoughts can be read electronically and printed out on a computer screen in word format. Also with DEW is the ability for your entire central nervous system to be monitored and *manipulated* along with your pulmonary system, lymphatic system, musculoskeletal system, and respiratory system. Your body is electric, so your body can also be controlled electronically from a remote point. Your thoughts, emotions, and even your dreams can be manipulated. So with microchip technology, the probability that you will no longer have a free will exists. Not to mention the fact that you will be able to be tracked and traced wherever you go. You will be an absolute slave.

If you think this is a little far fetched, let me tell you from personal experience it is not. I remember once being at work on the phone with a customer when I very uncharacteristically blurted out something inappropriate. It wasn't that what I said was bad, but it was in the wrong environment and the wrong situation. It stunned me. I know I was being electronically manipulated with DEW beyond a doubt. Likewise many Targeted Individuals have suffered from horrible tortures and rape because of these horrible weapons and those unconscionable people who use them.   And they are not all chipped.

So now imagine what your life could be like if your body and all of its functions were under the complete control of someone who did not at all have your best interests at heart, nor had any kind of moral or ethical code, nor any fear at all that there was a God who was going to hold him accountable for the way he treated you.   Your thoughts, emotions, and will are entirely under someone else's command.   You are no longer your own person. You are a slave.

I contend that this is entirely the design of this pandemic. It was planned in advance so says Dr. Fauci in 2017. The US Secretary of State, Mike Pompeo, called the pandemic a live exercise on CNN. The video was posted on YouTube March 24th at 6:24 am by Rebellious Legion. When Pompeo Makes the statement, Trump is standing by and remarks, "You should have let us know." Donald Trump in one of his recent public addresses admitted that this pandemic was artificially introduced. [22] It was designed to create a crisis that would instill fear. In that regard, because most American's don't understand what is happening, it has been successful. Fear is a weapon that is used to persuade you to cooperate. To deal with the crisis we have to accept certain measures to ensure our *safety*. So being given a vaccine that will in all probability cause harm to our bodies and also include a chip which will be used to control manipulate and exploit us is the *solution* to the crisis that was orchestrated by *them* anyway.

Now consider this. If the NWO wants to vaccinate and chip everyone so they can keep track of everyone, they have to reduce the world's population. Why do they have to reduce the world's population? For one thing, if they want to track every person on the planet, and they don't reduce the world's population, there would be entirely too much data to be processed and stored. I don't care how sophisticated your system is, that is a huge burden. So eliminating about 1/3 of the world's population is on the agenda.

Representing multiple fields of study, including ecology, agriculture, biology, and economics, the

---

22 Libby Cathey and Michelle Stoddart, Coronavirus government response updates: Trump says CDC now advising Americans to wear non-medical masks (ABC News, abcnews.go.com, April 3, 2020, 6:42 pm.

researchers told reporters that facts are facts: Humanity has far exceeded its sustainable population size, so either one in three humans can choose how they want to die themselves, or there can be some sort of government-mandated liquidation program—but either way, people have to start dying.[23]

As of September 2019, the UN Sustainable Development Goals no longer include any statement of population reduction. However, there is still a perceived need by some in power who are still pushing to reduce the world's population.[24]

Why is this so important to the New World Order? They want to significantly reduce the ability of the population to resist their domination and control. If they reduce the world's population, particularly very strong and intelligent people who can think independently and see right through their schemes as well as people they feel are genetically unfit, that will make the world an easier place for them to control.

In Revelation 9, the sixth trumpet is sounded and God unleashes angels who kill 1/3 of mankind. However, these are those who refused to repent of their misdeeds. *9:21 And they did not repent of their murders, nor of their witchcraft, nor of their fornications, nor of their thefts.*[25]

---

23 Scientists:'Look, One-Third of the Human Race Has to Die For Civilization To Be Sustainable, So How Do We Want To Do This?' (the Onion, www-theonion-com.cdn.ampproject.org, 1/26/12, 9:15 am
24 Kate Kelland, Correspondent, Reuters, Bill Gates has a warning about population growth, World Economic Forum, reform.org, Sept 19, 2018.
25Don Esposito. Hebraic Roots Bible (Kindle Location 43826). Congregation of YHWH Jerusalem. Kindle Edition).

6 Martial Law, FEMA, and the Church

Martial law will be one of the last stages of Project Blue Beam, and journalists have been predicting for years that martial law will be coming down the pike. If martial law is enacted, the Constitution will be suspended and all of our human and legal rights with it. There will be no reversal of the enactment of martial law. It is of course anticipated that there will be resistance among the populace. In preparation for this, FEMA began in 2016 training the *Clergy Response Team* to persuade Christians to cooperate under a perversion of the Romans 13 instruction to obey those in authority. Ultimately these pastors will be persuading their flocks to cooperate with being shuffled off to internment camps. Consider that this is exactly what happened to the Jews during the Holocaust. Eventually, they were shuffled to the ovens to be burned alive, thrown en mass into holes in the ground where they were buried alive or shuffled into gas chambers where they were gassed to death. In an article from Armageddon Times one pastor, Pastor Mansfield, who was invited to participate in the training was shocked by what he was hearing. The author of the article writes,

> *.. pastors will be utilized as informants. This violates the legal privilege of confidentiality between pastor and church-goer, that is currently recognized by law. All church-goers can no longer trust the sanctity of personal confessions and revelations made to pastors and priests. This one illegal act by DHS completely undermines the Christian Church in America! ... With a minimum of 28,000 pastors being a part of this dastardly plan, we need to all put our pastors under our watchful eye.*[26]

If the church has been compromised in this way, as well as the pastoral ministry, this will erode the trust which is a cornerstone of Christian ministry. To cooperate with something like this is to completely miss the point of being a shepherd of the Lord's sheep.

For most of my life, my church has been the center of my existence. I would have gladly done anything that was asked of me. I gave huge sums of money to my church, volunteered in multiple ministries and participated in small groups. Yet when I became a targeted individual, I found my church or any pastor that I reached out to to be completely unresponsive. One of my best friends, who has been tortured for 30 years as a targeted individual, approached her former pastor who told her that he could not help her unless he got permission from the governor. She is living in a shelter, she has very little money and she is dying of cancer due to constant attack by electromagnetic weapons. She has contacted the police and the FBI and has gotten no cooperation. If she had

---

26 28,000 Pastors Are Training To Keep You Calm On Your Way to a FEMACamp (<u>thearmageddontimes.com</u>, 2020).

done something criminal, this would still be illegal. If she had done something criminal she could be tried and, if convicted, assessed the *appropriate* penalty for her crime. She hasn't been charged with a crime. If she were convicted of murder, what is being done to her is *still* illegal. This is the manifestation of the spirit of lawlessness   and it appears that her pastor is cooperating!   What this says to me is that the dream that Yahweh gave me, when I didn't understand at the time, was indeed his message to me. The church is in trouble. Just as the church became corrupted in the 4th century by cooperating with the Roman Emperor, so now the church has become corrupted again by cooperating with the government.

Are we so comfortable and satisfied with our lives in this country, that we can't see the danger signs that something is very wrong in America? If I were a pastor and someone told me that I could not do something to help one of my parishioners, I would ask a lot of questions. If I am being told by a government official that I can't respond to someone's need, I would first consider the scripture and what Yahweh would ask of me.

In these times, as I am laid off work and the future is uncertain, and I am waiting and watching to see what will happen next, I am praying a prayer that I have learned to pray every day. "Search me and know me, and see if there be any wicked way in me. Try me and test me. Create in me a clean heart, oh God, and renew a right spirit in me." I pray for my friends who are being tortured and tormented daily, many of whom are believers. I am praying for any pastor I have ever known that in these times they will be honest with themselves and with Yahweh about the state of their soul. We need the spiritual leadership of this country to seriously examine themselves.   You cannot surrender the Lord's sheep to a monster. You cannot do it.

This country is under judgment right now. I know how desperately evil this nation has become. I'm a researcher. I see the shedding of innocent blood; the betrayal of innocent children by officials high up in government; the prostituting of minors and sexual exploitation of women; the lies, deception, and the destruction of innocent life. If ever there were a time that we need pastors to be on their toes, it's now. If ever there were a time for pastors to examine themselves, it's now. We are facing a monster in this country. You don't want to face a monster if your heart and motives are impure.

The body of believers needs to get behind their leadership. Positive encouragement and faithfulness is order here. We must sometimes challenge those in authority in the church. We have to do it, and we have to do it responsibly. Everybody in the body of believers has to take a leadership role when it comes to speaking up about corruption in America and our role as a body to stand against it. We have to be accountable and responsible ourselves for paying attention and responding. We can't wait for the pastor to do it for us. Remember those believers who stood up against Rome. Remember the price they paid. Remember those who translated the scripture into the common tongue of the people amidst opposition. They paid with their lives. Be prepared to stand with those who speak out. If the pastor loses his license to preach, we defend him. If the church loses its tax-exempt status, we put a little more in the plate. If people in our church lose their jobs for speaking up, we help out. We stand with them. We become a united front.

What Yahweh said when it all began for me was, "Hold fast to your confession of faith." I held on, and it was no small feat. Electromagnetic torture is nothing to take lightly. Those who tortured me were deliberately targeting my faith in Yahweh. They tormented me with depression topped with the horrible thought that Yahweh had abandoned me. The church would not listen to me. I was being constantly harassed at work and my home was being broken into. My car was being vandalized. I owned a Toyota Corolla. Those vehicles are known for longevity. As my mechanic brother repeatedly says, "Toyota's don't die." I owned the car for 19 years. When I finally gave the car to my brother it had 348,000 miles on it. In that amount of time, I made upwards of $18,000 in maintenance and repairs because of constant vandalism. I would come home and find my apartment had been broken into. On one occasion, I walked into my home and noticed immediately that something was wrong. I picked up my little dog and took him with me outside to my car as I called the police. When the police were finished, I went to get my dog out of the car. He didn't want to get out of the car. He ran from me. I went to the other side of the car to get him and he ran again. This is a very abnormal behavior for my dog. He was terrified. When I finally got him in my arms I had to hold him for a long time to get him to calm down. Where the culprits ever caught? Was anyone ever charged? Not to my knowledge. Yet, my home was broken into 4 times in five years. I held fast to my confession of faith.

As we speak, the Catholic Church is being sued by multiple victims of sexual abuse perpetrated by Catholic priests. Public officials such as Hillary Clinton known for their lawless acts are being brought, slowly albeit, to justice. Corrupted Child Protective Services agents are being brought to justice for trafficking in children. Though we still have journalists who tell the truth being jailed and even murdered. This is not a time for Christians to take up the "Don't worry, be happy" banner. This is no time for, "We're just gonna trust God and everything is gonna turn our all right," mantra. They said the same thing in Jeremiah's day before they went into exile.   We *should* trust God, at the same time we prepare to do battle.   It's a parring down time, and a time for self-examination.   It is a time for pastors behind the pulpit to speak the truth. We are in trouble! It is not going to get any better.   We have to come before Yahweh with broken and contrite spirits.

We look for the second coming, but not sitting on top of a hill wearing white robes. We do it in the streets as we do everything we can to rescue human lives and souls from the wreckage of a wayward government.

I am familiar with the scripture that talks about the wrath of Yahweh;

> Revelation 6:14-17 (HRB) And the heaven departed like a scroll being rolled up. And mountains and islands were moved out of their places. And the kings of the earth, and the great ones, and the commanders, and the powerful ones, and every slave, and every freeman hid themselves in the caves and in the rocks of the mountains. And "they said to the mountains and to the rocks, Fall on us," and hide us from the face of the One sitting on the throne, and from the wrath of the Lamb, because the great day of His wrath has come; and who is able to stand?

We as Americans and Christians need to consider something very dangerous. Our government has used our troops overseas to advance the interests of big business in this country. Every war that we have fought since my grandmother was born in 1906, was fought under false pretenses. The line we have been parroting for years is that "Our troops are over there fighting for our freedom." Okay, stop and think about how that works. They are over there, and we are here. While they are over there, *our freedoms are being systematically stripped from us by our own government*. At the same, time they are guilty of shedding innocent blood *over there* in the name of the United States of America. I am a veteran. I didn't sign up to kill innocent people, and I don't believe any soldier does. What he/she knows is what he/she is told and he/she knows to follow orders. In 2001 the 9/11 crisis was used as an excuse to arrest innocent people, commit terrible acts of abuse against innocent civilians, and deny them legal representation. This kind of thing has gone on in Iraq, Afghanistan, in South American countries, and poor third world nations for years. If we have a government that is willing to deceive us while in our name they are shedding innocent blood and stripping defenseless nations of their natural resources, and we are not addressing the problem as believers, God will address the problem. I am familiar with the intelligence community and how they operate. Considering that every country in the world has an intelligence branch, and considering that other countries are getting tired of the abuses heaped upon them by the US, there are no doubt spies all over this nation from every nation in the world, including Russia. Consider what would happen if a group of nations decided to attack this country in retaliation for the crimes committed against humanity by the US Government. This nation is a strong nation militarily speaking, but if she has lost favor with the Almighty, and someone decided to attack, his hand will not defend us. Yet, for the sake of the righteous, he might, if we do what we should be doing - holding our government accountable. The US has become very imperialist in its relationship to other weaker nations. We have used our advantage to supplant and exploit other countries that do not have the power to fight back. I would recommend reading *The Shock Doctrine*, by investigative journalist Naomi Klein, also *The Praetorian Guard* by former CIA Case Officer, John Stockwell, and *Guantanamo, What the World Should Know* by Michael Ratner of the National Lawyers Guild and Ellen Ray.

> *2 Chronicles 7:14 (HRB) …and My people, on whom My name is called, shall be humbled, and shall pray, and shall seek My face, and shall turn back from their evil ways, then I will hear from Heaven, and will forgive their sin, and will heal their land.*

7 When We Declared Independence

John Adams and the founding fathers fought hard to free the American colonists from tyranny. The colonists were being looted by King George, and they had no one to represent them in parliament. The colonists were being exploited for the sake of the already deep pockets of the wealthy in merry old England. They couldn't have cared less about the colonists themselves. They were expendable. Their lives didn't matter. So the colonists did the unthinkable. They declared independence on July 4th, 1776. The first paragraph of the declaration of independence reads;

The unanimous Declaration of the thirteen united States of America, When in the Course of human events, it becomes necessary for one people to dissolve the political bands which have connected them with another, and to assume among the powers of the earth, the separate and equal station to which the Laws of Nature and of Nature's God entitle them, a decent respect to the opinions of mankind requires that they should declare the causes which impel them to the separation.

Reading this paragraph, I am struck by one very important concept, the writers of this declaration needed to separate themselves from political ties with England to assert their equality which they were *entitled* to according to the *Laws of Nature* and *Nature's God*. The foundation of the Declaration of Independence is the understanding that God in his infinite wisdom made the colonists equal to those attempting to enslave them and profit from them. Let's read further;

We hold these truths to be self-evident, that all men are created equal, that they are endowed by their Creator with certain unalienable Rights, that among these are Life, Liberty and the pursuit of Happiness.--That to secure these rights, **Governments are instituted among Men, deriving their just powers from the consent of the governed,** --That whenever any Form of Government becomes destructive of these ends, it is the Right of the People to alter or to abolish it, and to institute new Government, laying its foundation on such principles and organizing its powers in such form, as to them shall seem most likely to effect their Safety and Happiness.

There it is again, this understanding that God created all men equal. It goes further in declaring that God has granted all men certain inalienable rights. What does that mean? First, we understand that God's authority in granting *inalienable rights* cannot be challenged or usurped. There is no authority higher than the authority of God. Therefore if God grants all whom he has created certain rights, they cannot be revoked by any other authority. The declaration goes further in saying that those that govern can do so only with the permission of the governed, and when the government oversteps their boundaries, we the people have the right to abolish it. That is a very strong statement. Let that sink in.

The next statement is very interesting. It speaks to our tendency to accommodate those who cause us to suffer rather than to work to stop them from so doing.

Prudence, indeed, will dictate that Governments long established should not be changed for light and transient causes; and accordingly all experience hath shewn, that mankind are more disposed to suffer, while evils are sufferable, than to right themselves by abolishing the forms to which they are accustomed.

In other words, we shouldn't and are not inclined to want to abolish the government at every whim. We are also inclined to endure rather than going through the pain of making necessary changes. Reading further, however, the writers speak of necessity. The Declaration lists the grievances which the colonists have against the King. There is much emotion packed into the following words.

But when a long train of abuses and usurpations, pursuing invariably the same Object evinces a design to reduce them under absolute Despotism, it is their right, it is their duty, to throw off such Government, and to provide new Guards for their future security.--Such has been the patient sufferance of these Colonies; and such is now the necessity which constrains them to alter their former Systems of Government. ***The history of the present King of Great Britain is a history of repeated injuries and usurpations, all having in direct object the establishment of an absolute Tyranny over these States. To prove this, let Facts be submitted to a candid world.***

He has refused his Assent to Laws, the most wholesome and necessary for the public good.

He has forbidden his Governors to pass Laws of immediate and pressing importance, unless suspended in their operation till his Assent should be obtained; and when so suspended, he has utterly neglected to attend to them.

He has refused to pass other Laws for the accommodation of large districts of people, *unless those people would relinquish the right of Representation in the Legislature,* a right inestimable to them and formidable to tyrants only.

He has called together legislative bodies at places unusual, uncomfortable, and distant from the depository of their public Records, for the sole purpose of fatiguing them into compliance with his measures.

He has dissolved Representative Houses repeatedly, for opposing with manly firmness his invasions on the rights of the people.

He has refused for a long time, after such dissolutions, to cause others to be elected; whereby the Legislative powers, incapable of Annihilation, have returned to the People at large for their exercise; *the State remaining in the mean time exposed to all the dangers of invasion from without, and convulsions within.*

He has endeavored to prevent the population of these States; for that purpose obstructing the Laws for Naturalization of Foreigners; refusing to pass others to encourage their migrations hither, and raising the conditions of new Appropriations of Lands.

He has obstructed the Administration of Justice, by

refusing his Assent to Laws for establishing Judiciary powers.

He has made Judges dependent on his Will alone, for the tenure of their offices, and the amount and payment of their salaries.

He has erected a multitude of New Offices, and sent hither swarms of Officers to harass our people, ***and eat out their substance.***

He has kept among us, in times of peace, Standing Armies without the Consent of our legislatures.

He has affected to render the Military independent of and superior to the Civil power. [In other words, the King made their military subordinate to him instead of to the colonists]

He has combined with others to subject us to a jurisdiction foreign to our constitution, and unacknowledged by our laws; giving his Assent to their Acts of pretended Legislation: [Did allow other countries to exploit them.]

For Quartering large bodies of armed troops among us:

For protecting them, by a mock Trial, from punishment for any Murders which they should commit on the Inhabitants of these States:

For cutting off our Trade with all parts of the world:

For imposing Taxes on us without our Consent:

For depriving us in many cases, of the benefits of Trial by Jury:

For transporting us beyond Seas to be tried for pretended offenses

For abolishing the free System of English Laws in a neighboring Province, establishing therein an Arbitrary government, and enlarging its Boundaries so as to render it at once an example and fit instrument for introducing the same absolute rule into these Colonies:

__For taking away our Charters, abolishing our most valuable Laws, and altering fundamentally the Forms of our Governments:__

__For suspending our own Legislatures, and declaring themselves invested with power to legislate for us in all cases whatsoever.__

__He has abdicated Government here, by declaring us out of his Protection and waging War against us.__

__He has plundered our seas, ravaged our Coasts, burnt our towns, and destroyed the lives of our people.__

He is at this time transporting large Armies of foreign Mercenaries to complete the works of death, desolation and tyranny, already begun with circumstances of cruelty & perfidy scarcely paralleled in the most barbarous ages, and totally unworthy the Head of a civilized nation.

__He has constrained our fellow Citizens taken Captive on the high Seas to bear Arms against their Country, to become the executioners of their friends and Brethren, or to fall themselves by their Hands.__

__He has excited domestic insurrections amongst us, and has endeavored to bring on the inhabitants of our frontiers, the merciless Indian Savages, whose known rule of warfare, is an undistinguished destruction of all ages, sexes and conditions.__

In sum, King George stripped them of all ability to advocate for themselves in parliament. Any laws they enacted he abolished. He ignored laws that he permitted to be enacted if they got in his way. Their judges were dependent on the King because their paychecks would be revoked if they didn't satisfy him. He transported them across the sea to stand trial for false allegations. He deliberately incited riots among them. He established standing armies among them without their consent, and they were required to provide them room and board. He taxed them without their consent. He refused to hold his armies accountable for acts committed against the colonists, including murder, by establishing mock trials and exonerating his soldiers for their criminal acts. (Can you see the parallels here with what happened in Guantanamo and Abu Ghraib?) Their own military was subject not to them, but to the King of England. As their King, he was obliged to protect them, and instead declared they were out of his protection and began waging war against them. (A war is being waged today against private citizens by gangstalkers all over the world.) He even took captive colonists on the high seas and forced them to kill their own friends and fellow colonists. He stirred up colonists against other colonists and also brought the Indians against them. (More parallels here with ISIS, ANTIFA and Black Lives Matter and the rioting since the death of George Floyd.) At the time the Declaration was signed, the King was bringing armies against them. They had no choice but to fight to defend themselves.

Let's finish reading.

> In every stage of these Oppressions We have Petitioned for Redress in the most humble terms: Our repeated Petitions have been answered only by repeated injury. A Prince whose character is thus marked by every act which may define a Tyrant, is unfit to be the ruler of a free people.

Nor have We been wanting in attentions to our British brethren. We have warned them from time to time of attempts by their legislature to extend an unwarrantable jurisdiction over us. We have reminded them of the circumstances of our emigration and settlement here. **We have appealed to their native justice and magnanimity, and we have conjured them by the ties of our common kindred to disavow these usurpations, which, would inevitably interrupt our connections and correspondence. They too have been deaf to the voice of justice and of consanguinity. We must, therefore, acquiesce in the necessity, which denounces our Separation, and hold them, as we hold the rest of mankind, Enemies in War, in Peace Friends.**

We, therefore, the Representatives of the united States of America, in General Congress, Assembled, appealing to the Supreme Judge of the world for the rectitude of our intentions, do, in the Name, and by Authority of the good People of these Colonies, solemnly publish and declare, That these United Colonies are, and of Right ought to be Free and Independent States; that they are Absolved from all Allegiance to the British Crown, and that all political connection between them and the State of Great Britain, is and ought to be totally dissolved; and that as Free and Independent States, they have full Power to levy War, conclude Peace, contract Alliances, establish Commerce, and to do all other Acts and Things which Independent States may of right do. ***And for the support of this Declaration, with a firm reliance on the protection of divine Providence, we mutually pledge to each other our Lives, our Fortunes and our sacred Honor.***

Holding themselves accountable to their Creator, those assembled in congress declared they had made every effort to respect the British Crown and work with those ruling over them to come to agreements civilly and respectably. The British Crown responded with hostility, refusal to listen, compromise, or in any way cooperate with the colonists. That is because the British Crown saw the colonists not as people, but as the property of the British State and therefore slaves with no rights at all. Their motivation was entirely business-related. They wanted to profit from the colonists' business transactions whether or not it was profitable or beneficial to the colonists. The well being and welfare of the colonists had no bearing at all on the Parliament's political policies. That, my fellow Americans, is absolute despotism and tyranny. When we declared independence, we had no choice but to fight to preserve our lives. We fought and we won the revolutionary war. However, over the two centuries that America has been a nation, covert forces with a private agenda have been fighting to return us to a state of despotism. Once again, **_we have no choice_** but to fight again to preserve our lives and our futures.

Author Naomi Wolf who wrote *The End of America,* observes that freedom is not an evergreen tree. Central governments repeatedly decline toward tyranny. Preserving our freedom is the same as preserving our lives. The lives of America's children and the rest of our citizenry is at risk. A pervasive atheistic, nihilistic, socialistic mindset is dominating the power centers of America. Increasingly our civil liberties are being dismantled and constitutional rights ignored or nullified altogether. Being alert and prepared to confront this darkness will result in restraining the darkness until the return of Jesus Christ. It is our right and our responsibility to take a stand.

8 Responsible Americans

More than a year ago, a Racine County Wisconsin Sheriff, Trip Castor, took a stand.   He did what I wish all Americans would do.   He remembered who he was, and he reminded his listeners what America is about. At a public meeting he went on record stating the following;

> The last time I read the Declaration of Independence it simply reminds all of us that we are endowed by our creator with certain inalienable rights, that means God-given, among these life, liberty, and the pursuit of happiness, and the governments were instituted among men specifically to secure our God-given rights, and it says when governments become destructive to these ends, meaning when they go above and beyond trying to secure our liberties [to] trying to take them, it's the right of the people to alter or to abolish that government either by voting or ultimately, God forbid, by using our second amendment rights to protect ourselves from tyranny.[27]

27 YouTube Video posted by aplanetruth4u Sheriffs Begin Resisting Tyrannical Government. Posted April 25th, 2020

Unfortunately, though the Sheriff presented his statements in a rational and respectful manner, he lost his job.

In 1993 a former Youngstown Ohio Sheriff turned congressman, Jim Traficant, exposed the illegal bankruptcy of the United States Government in Congress.[28] The bankruptcy was declared in 1933 as a result of debts incurred during WWI. The gold standard was abrogated. It was declared then that the government of the United States existed in name only. The entire country, lock, stock, and barrel including all the citizens present and future, were surrendered to the Federal Reserve in repayment of the debt owed to the international bankers. This was covered up and not reported to the American people. Our income taxes were allegedly created for the purpose of repaying the debt. The people of America became a commodity. It should be noted that 1933 was the same year that Hitler was declared the Chancellor of Germany.

Ironically, Jim Traficant was subsequently charged with tax evasion and sent to prison for two years. He was released from prison. In 2014 he was operating a tractor on his farm and had a seizure which resulted in a fatal accident.

During the 9/11 crisis, which we have already discussed was an inside job, Muslim peoples in Afghanistan and Iraq as well as the US were arrested, held without being charged, sodomized, and otherwise tortured in US-controlled prisons. MP guard, SP4 Joseph M. Darby, Master-at-Arms First Class William J. Kimbro, 1LT David O. Sutton, 229th MP Company, refused to perpetuate the abuse and did the proper thing in reporting the abuse.

Dr. Ngozi Ezike and Minnesota Senator Scott Jensen

---

28 Frederick-Earl, The US Government went Bankrupt in 1933 and is No
    Longer a Republic. (© Family Guardian Fellowship, famguardian.org).

faithfully reported to the American people that the figures for COVID-19 related deaths are being inflated. Considering that the US public media owned by six corporations that are also controlling our government are *not* faithfully reporting the truth, we are grateful to the numerous journalists working for offbeat news reporting agencies consistently doing their best to tell the American people the truth. We are also aware that a number of journalists who have exposed corruption and corrupted public officials have ended up in jail or are murdered or died under suspicious circumstances.

During this Corona crisis, multiple Sheriff's have been refusing to enforce the shelter in place order citing the constitution. Among those were Riverside County Sheriff Chad Bianco[29]; Michigan Sheriff's Mike Borkovich, Ted Schendel, Ken Falk, and Kim Cole[30]; and Snohomish County Washington Sheriff Adam Fortney.[31] In addition, South Dakota Governor, Kristi Noem, refused to close down her state in response to the COVID-19 crisis.[32] The Wisconsin Supreme Court ruled the stay at home order was an attack on American civil liberties and tossed it.[33] Shelly Luther, a Dallas Salon Owner, was sentenced to 7 days in jail and fined $7000 for defying the governor's order and reopening her business[34] while Texas residents staged a

---

29 Pat Droney, Report: California sheriff refuses to enforce Newsom's stay at home orders (lawenforcementtoday.com, May 11, 2020).
30 Tristan Justice, Four Michigan Sheriffs Say They Won't Enforce Governor's Totalitarian Orders (Federalist, the federalist.com, April 15, 2020).
31 Zoe Nemerever, Why 'Constitutionalist sheriffs' won't enforce coronavirus restrictions (The Washington Post, washingtonpost.com.cdn.ampproject.org, April 23, 2020).
32 Daniel Villarreal, South Dakota Throws Parade for Governor Kristi Noem Who Declined to Shut Her State Amid Pandemic (Newsweek online, 4/28/2020 at 6:25 pm).
33 Joaquin Flores, Deep-State Foiled: Wisconsin Ends COVID-19 Tyranny - Supreme Court Tosses Lockdown Order. (fort-fuss.com, May 14, 2020.
34 Jessica Chasmar, Dallas salon owner sentenced to week in jail for reopening

protest against the lockdown and brandished signs like *Texas will not take the Mark of the Beast.*[35] In addition to that, United States Attorney General, Bill Bar, is threatening state Governors with legal action if they continue with lockdown orders after the crisis has passed. This is a bit controversial as it infringes on the right of state governors to exercise control over their jurisdictions. Barr insists he will support citizens who sue their states.[36]

These are responsible Americans. Responsible Americans were present at the signing of the Declaration of Independence. They were prepared to fight for their freedom. There are still Americans who understand what it means to be an American. Responsible Americans don't just follow the leader like lemmings jumping over a cliff. Responsible Americans tell the truth. Responsible Americans take a stand and say no to government bullies. Responsible Americans understand what that Constitution is for, and responsible Americans are not afraid to face down a deceitful and corrupted government. Responsible Americans, like Trip Castor, understand that in order to preserve freedom we have to make sacrifices and stand up for the truth. Trip Castor, I'm proud of you. You make me so proud, I could cry.

What we as Americans are afraid of is losing our jobs, not having money to pay the bills, mortgage, car note, credit card, etc. We want to maintain our standard of living. Early Americans knew they would have no life to maintain if they did not stand up and fight.

---

business, refuses to apologize (The Washington Times, washingtontimes.com, May 6, 2020.)

35 Phil McCausland, Protesters in Texas, other states demand end to lockdowns day after Trump's 'LIBERATE' tweets (NBC News, nbcnews.com, April 18, 2020, 5:34 pm).

36 Jason Easley, Barr Threatens to Sue States That Keep Stay at Home Order in Place (POLITICUSUSA, politicususa.com, April 21st, 2020).

The spiritual leaders in this nation need to rethink their position. Is the government going to threaten to revoke their licenses to preach, tax-exempt status, etc if they don't cooperate? Probably. What does the scripture say, "Thou shalt have no other gods before me."   But the scripture says we should be obedient to those in authority, for there is no authority that is not ordained by God. Romans 13:1-2 says;

Let every soul be subject to the higher authorities, for there is no authority except from Elohim, but the existing authorities have been ordained by YAHWEH. So that the one resisting the civil authority has opposed the ordinance of Elohim, and the ones opposing will receive judgment to themselves (HRB).

However, when this verse is preached, Hosea 8:4 is ignored which says *They have set up kings, but not by Me. They have made rulers, but I did not know (HRB).* The problem is that we do not understand Yahweh's intent. Social order is important for the good of all. When social order is disrupted, it is up to civil authorities to restore order.   However, we have to understand that in the United States, *we the people are the government.* We also have to understand that those in positions of power and authority have laws that govern the execution of their power. When they violate those laws they have stepped outside of the bounds of their authority. When we declared independence, we knew that governments have a habit of going astray, and our constitution allowed for we the people to depose a government that had overstepped their boundaries.   That is why Yahweh himself deposes authorities.

Isaiah 3:12-14 As for My people, children are their oppressors, and women rule over him. Oh My people, those leading you cause you to go astray, and they swallow the way of your paths. YAHWEH stands up to plead His cause, and stands up to judge the peoples. YAHWEH will enter into judgment with the elders of His people and their kings. For you have eaten up the vineyard, the plunder of the poor is in your houses (HRB).

When we talk about inalienable rights endowed by God, we are saying they are God-given and *irrevocable*. Yet, our government has committed murder, lied to the American public, violated our Constitution, falsely accused innocent people such as the victims of Abu Ghraib and Guantanamo and committed acts of atrocity against them *to cover up their own crimes*. Go ahead and google the words, "found dead" and see how many hits you get. A rising number of Journalists who are trying to expose government corruption are also among those "found dead."

Have I discussed yet the trillions of dollars that have come up missing from the Pentagon? The day before the 9/11 event, Donald Rumsfeld announced that 2.3 trillion dollars were *missing* from the Pentagon. Interestingly, the area where the missile (not a plane as reported in the official story) hit was the auditor's office which is on the opposite side of the building where one would expect. It also required considerable maneuvering to make that hit when the other side of the building would have been an easier target. If you are a terrorist, you wouldn't have aimed at the auditor's office. You would aim for the offices of the military command chiefs which would have been easier for a *plane* or a missile to hit. The records of the audit, created by those attempting to trace the missing funds, were destroyed - by a bomb as reported by the auditor who was a witness to the event. She logged into her computer and the bomb went off.[37]

Let's consider how much of this Yahweh is going to endure while the believing sector of the country stands by in obedience to their authority. We are *we the people. We are the boss.* When you have an employee who lies to you, steals from you, and even commits murder while trying to blame innocent people, you fire them, and when you fire them you stop paying them! Then you prosecute them. They broke the law!!

Fortunately, there are people like Tom Fitton of the American Center for Law and Justice who are going after corruption. US Attorney General Bill Barr is fighting for our constitution.

Responsible Americans fight back! So, it is the job of the spiritual leadership of this country to stand up and fight with those who fight injustice. God ordained the church to fight! Consider that in the old testament, the priesthood was the criminal justice system. That's right. If a crime was committed, it was the priest's job to investigate the crime and execute justice (Deut. 21:5). God is never on the side of oppressive governments. He stands for the weak and the righteous. If he didn't, Rome would never have fallen. If he didn't, America would never have been born. God is always a defender of the weak. He will not defend the wicked.

Our problem is that our nation is no longer a united front. Unifying this nation to take a stand against a corrupt government would be extremely difficult. However, as believers in Jesus Christ, it is our job to be a light. We cannot condone what our government is doing. We can't just brush it off. Our pulpits should be burning with fury. We can take a

---

37 David Ray Griffin, The New Pearl Harbor Revisited: The Cover-up and the Expose (Northampton: Olive Branch Press, 2008) 73.

stand against abortion, against gay marriage, against pedophilia and safe sex. Should we not also take a stand against a government that lies, steals, and commits murder?

Something else that concerns me is the US Military. Every soldier in the US Military needs to understand what is going on here. If you are going to serve your country, that means that when you are ordered to do something that violates the US Constitution, you are under obligation to resist because it is *not* a lawful order. You took an oath to defend your country against all enemies both foreign and *domestic*. We have a domestic enemy.

As Christians, we lead the march of resistance against a corrupt government. We do it with Christlike attitudes and behavior. We don't use violence until it becomes absolutely necessary. We don't fire unless we are fired upon. The colonists, remember, had to take up arms to defend themselves. Jesus advised his disciples to carry a sword (Luke 22:36).We are respectful, compassionate, and merciful of those of the opposite opinion, but we stand firm. If Yahweh will avert this disaster, is because of and for the sake of the righteous.

We don't want them to declare martial law. We will be playing right into their hands. Even if it is one American at a time in whatever profession who stands up and says, "I can't and won't do this. This is wrong." It is our responsibility to defend people like Trip Castor. He very responsibly exercised his right to free speech. It is a violation of the law to fire a man for exercising his constitutional rights. If ever there is something we need to be willing to fight for, it is our right to free speech. When our neighbor's right to free speech is violated, we are under biblical and civil obligations to defend him.

9 Donald Trump and Corona

My mother voted for Trump. I didn't. I didn't vote for Hillary either. I voted for one of those other candidates who surrendered her votes to Hilary Clinton much to my chagrin. I lost faith in the presidency long ago. The problem is that every president since John F. Kennedy has been a puppet of the NWO.   In this country, big business and the United States Government have a very unholy alliance.   There is this revolving door between corporate American and Washington DC. We go to the polls and vote while corporate America goes to Washington and lobbies. They have money. We don't have that kind of money. Their money pays for campaign costs. Not every politician out there is committed to the NWO agenda, but most of them are.

Donald Trump is an interesting character. He is trying, I believe, to serve the American public without becoming a puppet of the NWO. However, he is surrounded by seasoned politicians who are NWOers.   I can tell you that they are determined to forward their agenda regardless of what it takes. If that means bullying, threatening, blackmailing, hypnotizing, or even assassinating the president to get what they want out of the oval office, they will do it. When I look at Donald Trump, I see a man who wants very much to be faithful to his office, but he is between a rock and a hard spot.   The fact that Nancy Pelosi went after him so venomously is highly indicative of the fact that he is *not* one of their puppets. The other thing that tells me that he is trying to do the right thing, is that he is petitioning for contributions from the American public so that he can further the cause of democracy in America. He regularly meets the public face to face and he regularly polls his constituents to get a feel for what they are thinking.

He has made some mistakes.   I am not in favor of building a wall.   I think that would be a mistake.   I was also horribly dismayed when he separated the children of illegal immigrants from their parents at the border.   The thought of it made my heart break, and I was terrified for those children.   I wanted to get in Trump's face for that, and rumors circulated that some of those children did not get returned to their parents and ended up being confiscated by trafficking rings operating in the US. I answered one of his polls, and I told him exactly what I thought about that. Trump's problem is that he is not a seasoned politician.   He's a small-town guy that made it big. He isn't evil, but some of his tactics are highly questionable.

When it came to Corona I was so hoping he would see right through this. Don't be surprised if we learn that those who surround Trump kept important information from him, deceived him or led him astray.   The fact that the Secretary of State, Pompeo called the pandemic a "live exercise" while Trump said quietly as he stood at his elbow, "You should have told us," would indicate things going on in Washington that are kept hidden from our President. He admitted in an offbeat remark that the pandemic was artificially induced. In the context that he said it, it was almost if he was trying to get it in there before someone tried to delete it from his speech. On May 19th, he went public saying that he was taking the malaria drug, Hydroxychloroquine as a preventative measure.   He had been promoting the use of this drug for two months. It has been on the list of essential medicines for 70 years and has been used effectively against the Coronavirus around the globe. Yet the FDA said it can cause heart problems.   Did it cause heart problems when it was used to treat Malaria? So pressure was put on President Trump obviously to promote the use of the vaccine.   Dr. Fauci admits that there is no guarantee that the vaccine will work and it could make things worse. His former associate, Dr. Judy Mikovits, says the vaccine will kill millions of people, though it will mean billions of dollars in profits for people like Fauci, Gates,   and the pharmaceutical companies that make it. So Trump has switched gears and reported that he will send the US Military door to door to distribute the vaccine. He didn't say we would be forced to take it, but when someone shows up at your door wearing a military uniform and carrying a gun, it demonstrates a threat of force.

What this tells me is that Trump needs courage, and he needs people around him who are not Washington bureaucrats. He is a sitting duck up there. Washington can be ruthless when it comes to promoting the NWO agenda.

I think we have an opportunity to communicate with our President that we support him. We need to pray diligently for him because, as I said, his good intentions can be supplanted by ruthless bureaucrats. I honestly feel bad for him. He is in many ways, though a very wealthy businessman, just a home town kinda guy surrounded by fat cats and bureaucrats who want to manipulate and railroad him.   It's tough because those people are wealthy, powerful, and determined to get their way. I have heard a lot of rotten things said about Trump, and I have seen a lot of good in the man.   Politics are ruthless.   Trump is not ruthless. He needs the King of Kings and Lord of Lords in that oval office with him.

10 King of Kings and Lord of Lords

*The earth is the Lord's and all that is in it, the world and those
who live in it - Psalms 24:1 NRSV
Our God is in the heavens, he does whatever he pleases, Psalms
115:3 NRSV*

The last President that tried to be faithful to the
American people, John F. Kennedy, was assassinated. They
tried to assassinate Andrew Jackson too because he kicked the
Federal Reserve out. They weren't able to nail Jackson.
Kennedy revoked the use of Federal Reserve currency and
reestablished the dollar made by the US Treasury as well. That
is another reason why they wanted him dead. People in high
places are regularly bribed, blackmailed, threatened, bullied,
and intimidated into cooperating with the NWO agenda. But I
know who sits on the throne, who was and is and is to come. I
know who puts a king on his throne and who takes him down.

The throne of Jesus Christ is firmly established. His
throne is invincible and unchallenged. He cannot be bribed,
blackmailed, threatened, or intimidated. They tried to kill him,

but he came out of that grave.   He is the King to whom we will all give an account.

And before him no creature is hidden, but all are naked and laid bare to the eyes of the one to whom we must render an account. Hebrews 4:13 (HRB).

It is a choice we all have to make. Sometimes doing the right thing costs us. I think about what it will cost me to make the wrong choice. This world is passing away. There will be an eternal kingdom established by Jesus Christ one day, and those who chose him to obey him will live for eternity in that Kingdom.   In his kingdom, there will be no hunger, no bloodshed, no stealing, no lying, no loneliness, no sickness, and no death. There will be no injustice in his Kingdom. No one will get away with murder in the Kingdom of Heaven.

Jesus Christ died to save you from your sins. If you get down on your knees and call on his name he will save you for all eternity.   You confess your sins to him, and they are forgiven. He won't use your wrongdoing to blackmail you or control you. He may require an earthly penalty of you for some infractions, but he is merciful, and your soul will be secure.

He loves you deeply and profoundly. His love never fails. He won't change his mind about you. He won't betray you. He won't forsake you. You will suffer in this life, as he did when he walked this earth, but your suffering will be rewarded in the next life. Be prepared to face persecution as we draw near to the end of this earthly kingdom, but hold fast to him. He will surely come through for you.

Luke 10:19 (Hebrew Roots Bible) Behold I give authority to you to tread on snakes and scorpions and all the power of the enemy, and nothing will harm you.